India

Come on a journey of discovery

Elaine Jackson

QED Publishing

Copyright © QED Publishing 2004

First published in the UK in 2004 by
QED Publishing
A Quarto Group Company
226 City Road
London, EC1V 2TT

www.qed-publishing.co.uk

A Catalogue record for this book is available
from the British Library.

ISBN 1 84538 293 5

Written by Elaine Jackson
Designed by Starry Dog Books Ltd
Editor: Christine Harvey
Maps by PCGraphics (UK) Ltd

Creative Director: Louise Morley
Editorial Manager: Jean Coppendale

Picture credits

Key: t = top, b = bottom, m = middle, c = centre,
l = left, r = right

Corbis Amit Bhargara 23m,/ Sheidan Collins 24,/
David Cumming 19t,/ Bennett Dean 22,/ David H.
Wells 25t,/ Blaine Harrington III 27t,/ Chris Hellier 27b,/
Robert Holmes 15m, 17t,/ Jeremy Horner 13,/ Earl
Kowall 18m, 18b, 24t,/ Caroline Penn 17b,/ Christian
Simonpietri 6–7;
Getty Glen Allison title page, 2t, 14b,/ Nicholas
VeVore 25b,/ Mark Downey 16–17,/ Ben Edwards
15t,/ Ingo Jezierski 2b,/ Santokh Kochar 2m, 7t,/
Phillip Lee Harvey 26b,/ Chris Noble 7b,/ Slede Preis
9b, 17m,/ Martin Puddy 8–9,/ Herb Schmitz 22–23,/
David Sutherland 20–21,/ Art Wolfe 21t;
Greta Jensen 9br, 10–11, 11tr, 23tl.

International and regional boundaries in areas of
dispute and conflict are shown as a simplification
of the true situation. This simplification has been
undertaken because this book is aimed at the
7–11 age group.

Printed and bound in China

Words in **bold** can be
found in the glossary
on page 28.

Contents

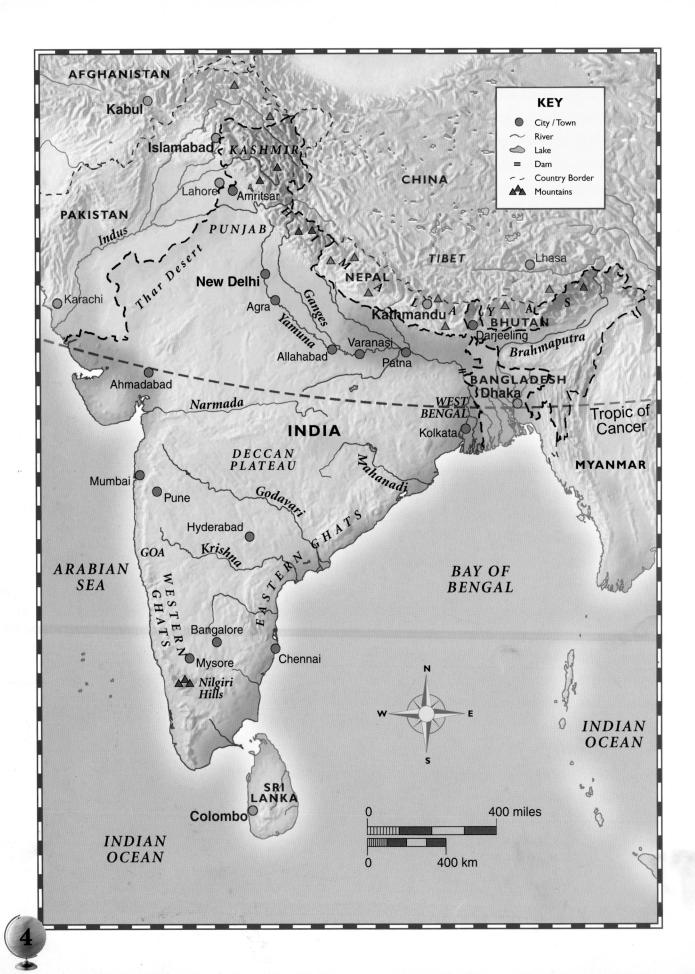

AFGHANISTAN

Kabul

Islamabad

KASHMIR

CHINA

Lahore

Amritsar

PAKISTAN

Indus

PUNJAB

Thar Desert

New Delhi

Karachi

Agra

Ganges

Yamuna

Allahabad

Varanasi

Patna

TIBET

Lhasa

NEPAL

Kathmandu

H I M A L A Y A S

Darjeeling

BHUTAN

Brahmaputra

BANGLADESH

Dhaka

Ahmadabad

Narmada

WEST BENGAL

Tropic of Cancer

INDIA

Kolkata

MYANMAR

DECCAN PLATEAU

Mahanadi

Mumbai

Pune

Godavari

Hyderabad

Krishna

GOA

WESTERN GHATS

EASTERN GHATS

ARABIAN SEA

BAY OF BENGAL

Bangalore

Mysore

Chennai

Nilgiri Hills

N

W   E

S

INDIAN OCEAN

SRI LANKA

Colombo

INDIAN OCEAN

KEY

●	City / Town
～	River
◯	Lake
=	Dam
- - -	Country Border
▲▲	Mountains

0   400 miles

0   400 km

Where in the world is India?

▲ The national flag of India

India lies in the southern part of the **continent** of Asia. India is surrounded by the Arabian Sea to the west, the Bay of Bengal to the east, the Indian Ocean to the south and the mountains of the Himalayas to the north (see map). India has borders with Bangladesh, Pakistan and several other countries.

India has a huge population. More than a billion (1 000 000 000) people live in India. That is nearly one-sixth of all the human beings on Earth! This makes India the world's second most heavily populated nation after China.

▼ India and its place in the world.

India

Did you know?

Name Republic of India
Location Southern Asia
Surrounding countries
Bangladesh, Pakistan, Nepal, Afghanistan, Sri Lanka, Tibet, Bhutan
Surrounding seas and oceans
Arabian Sea, Bay of Bengal, Indian Ocean
Length of coastline 5630km long
Capital New Delhi
Area 3 287 263km^2
Population 1 030 000 000
Life expectancy Male: 57, Female: 58
Religions Hinduism (80%), Islam (14%), Christianity, Sikhism, Buddhism, Jainism
Languages Official languages: Hindi and English. There are also 15 other different regional languages
Climate Tropical monsoon
Highest mountain range Himalayas
Major rivers Ganges (length: 2478km), Indus (length: 2897km), Brahmaputra (length: 2897km)
Currency Rupee

What is India like?

A land of contrasts

Travelling through India, you might think that it feels like two separate countries: **rural** India and **urban** India. Tens of millions of people live in very poor conditions in villages, where the ways of farming and growing food have not changed over hundreds of years. At the same time, sprawling Indian cities are thriving with modern, high-tech **industries.**

▼ The shops in Indian cities are packed one on top of the other, selling everything from suits to tongue scrapers!

Travelling across the landscape

The physical landscape of India is also varied. In the north there are the mountain ranges of the Himalayas. Here are some of the world's highest mountain peaks and the largest areas under snow outside the polar regions.

South of the Himalayas is the huge, flat area of land through which the mighty River Ganges flows. Southern India is an area of high, flat land called the Deccan Plateau. This has mountain ranges on either side, called the Eastern and Western Ghats.

▼ Many of India's rural areas are poor, and farmers stick to the slow but sure traditional farming methods.

A mixed climate

India's climate is very mixed. Travelling around the country, you will feel cold in the mountainous areas, which have snow all year round, then hot in the dry areas of arid desert, where there is little or no rainfall. Most of the rain falls in one season only, in four months during the summer.

The meaning of the flag

The orange stripe of the Indian flag stands for courage and sacrifice. The white stripe stands for truth, purity and peace, and the green for faith and growth. The symbol in the centre is called the Wheel of Ashoka – the wheel of law or progress.

▼ The snow-capped Himalayas are in northern India.

Climate – travelling through the seasons

The cooler months

Most of India has a tropical climate with three main seasons.

If you travel to India during the cooler months, between October and March, you will notice the hot dry winds that blow overland, crossing India from northeast to southwest.

The wetter months

If you travel in the summer months, June to September, you will experience the **monsoon** winds. They blow from the south west and sweep across the country. They reach India from the Indian Ocean and carry a lot of water with them. You will notice how unusual the monsoon winds are, because the rain that falls from them is very heavy, the drops are very large and the rain feels hot on your skin.

▼ Everyday life carries on as normal in India, even when the streets are flooded after the monsoon rains.

CLIMATIC DATA FOR MUMBAI (BOMBAY)

	Jan	Feb	March	April	May	June	July	Aug	Sept	Oct	Nov	Dec
Temperature (°C)	24	25	27	30	29	26	26	27	28	26	26	25
Rainfall (mm)	2	2	2	0	8	450	750	350	250	80	8	2

INDIA'S THREE SEASONS

Months	Temperature	Rainfall
October to March	Cool 24–25°C	Dry: Less than 10mm per month
April and May	Hot 28–31°C	Dry: Below 30mm per month
June to September	Hot 27–29°C	Very wet: over 600mm per month

June to September

ASIA
*HOT AIR
LOW PRESSURE*

INDIA

Arabian Sea

Bay of Bengal

Equator 0¡

INDIAN OCEAN

October to March

ASIA
*DENSE COLD AIR
HIGH PRESSURE*

INDIA

Arabian Sea

Bay of Bengal

Equator 0¡

INDIAN OCEAN

◄ The red arrows show which way the winds blow across India during the wet and cool seasons.

Learn about Geeta

❓ In July, Geeta will visit her grandparents in Mumbai (Bombay). What sort of clothes will she need to take?

❓ Geeta lives in Manchester in the UK. How would the rainfall in Mumbai at this time be similar to, or different from, the rainfall in Manchester?

Travelling through the countryside

Village life

Two thirds of the population of India live in villages. Travelling through villages, you will see people farming small plots of land. You will notice the whole family working on the land, including children. Many children in India cannot afford to go to school and less than half of the population of India can read and write.

Farm work

In the countryside, farming is often done by hand. Most farmers do not have enough money to buy tractors and so use traditional farming methods dating back hundreds of years. Many villages have no running water or **sewage** facilities, so diseases are still a problem in rural areas.

Cows

Cows, **oxen** and buffaloes are very important in Indian village life. Often, their horns are brightly painted to show that they are owned by a particular family. Cows' milk and other produce (such as butter, cheese and yoghurt) are an important food source for village people. The cow is **sacred** in the Hindu religion and its meat is never eaten. Cow dung is traditionally used as both a fertilizer and as a fuel.

▼ Families work hard on their farms. Women and girls help with weeding and harvesting the crops, as well as milking the animals, fetching water, preparing meals and looking after the smaller children.

▲ Farmers in India cannot usually afford modern farm machinery and use oxen and water buffaloes to pull their ploughs and carts. Any produce that the family does not need is taken by cart to market ('haat') to sell or exchange for other goods.

Extract from Suribi's diary
Suribi keeps a diary about life in her village

I am ten years old. I live in Chembakolli in south India. Every day I help my mother to fetch water from the well and to cook. We cook outside in our courtyard on a gas burner. I look after my little brother and sister, our cow and two goats. I make fuel by mixing cow dung with straw and leaving it to dry. I go to school for three hours each day, unless I am needed to work on the land.

Travelling through the farming areas

◀ Pile upon pile of top-quality fruit and vegetables are sold at small, open stalls.

The farming year in India is linked to the monsoon rain cycle. Farming varies from region to region, and depends on the climate, soil and landscape.

The north west

Our journey through the farming areas begins in Ladakh, where barley, cabbages and potatoes grow well. Fruit and rice are grown in Kashmir. Wheat, sugar, rice, potatoes and pulses are grown in the rich plains of Punjab.

Around the River Ganges

The huge plain of the River Ganges is India's main cereal growing area, producing wheat, rice, maize and pulses. Many fruits (such as lemons, apples, tomatoes), vegetables (including cauliflowers, aubergines, spinach) and spices are grown here.

The north east

India is the world's biggest **exporter** of tea. It is grown on huge plantations on the northern plains of Assam and Darjeeling. It is grown where there is heavy rainfall, good drainage and the land is **terraced** to prevent **soil erosion**. Many workers are needed to prepare the land, to weed the plantations and to pick the leaves from the bushes.

Central India

Travelling through the centre of India you will see fields of cotton, oil seeds and food grains, such as millet. Rice and sugar cane are grown in the coastal regions of the south and east because the climate is wetter there. Basmati rice is grown in the foothills of the Himalayas. Rice production is labour intensive and most of the work is done by hand.

The south

You will see coconut palms all over southern India. Rubber trees, spices, coffee, bananas and cashew nuts are also grown here for export.

▼ The tea leaves are placed in a basket strapped to the worker's back.

Did you know?
Most of the rice grown every year in India is eaten within the country, except basmati rice, which is exported.

Amazing, but true!
In 2001, India produced 22.5 per cent of the world's rice and was the second biggest producer after China.

▼ This map shows the main areas where food produce is grown.

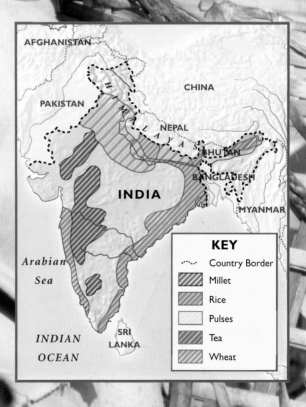

AFGHANISTAN

CHINA

PAKISTAN

H I M A L A Y A S

NEPAL

BHUTAN

BANGLADESH

INDIA

MYANMAR

Arabian Sea

INDIAN OCEAN

SRI LANKA

KEY

- - - - Country Border
Millet
Rice
Pulses
Tea
Wheat

A city tour of India

Mumbai (Bombay)

Mumbai (Bombay) is often referred to as India's 'city of dreams'. It is India's largest city and port. Mumbai is also India's leading industrial city. Cotton textiles, machinery, chemicals and cars are all manufactured there.

Mumbai is also the centre of India's film industry – 'Bollywood' – producing more films than any other place in the world. Visiting the city, you will see huge houses and great wealth, but also poor **slums** full of shacks and street children.

New Delhi

New Delhi is the capital city of India. It is an important business centre with many banks and offices. There are also factories manufacturing electronics, electrical appliances, chemicals, textiles and car parts.

Kolkata

Kolkata is India's second largest city. It is an industrial centre and major port. As in other Indian cities, wealth exists beside deep poverty, unemployment and overcrowding.

▲ Posters for 'Bollywood' movies are usually colourful and dramatic, just like the films.

A Mumbai child

Deepi is 12 years old and lives with her parents and brother in a large house in Mumbai. Deepi's father is a scientist. He works in the chemical industry, making medicines. Her mother is a teacher. Deepi and her brother attend school every day and Deepi wants to be a doctor when she grows up.

► Kolkata's slums are home to many street children.

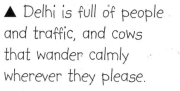

▲ Delhi is full of people and traffic, and cows that wander calmly wherever they please.

Bangalore

Bangalore in south central India is regarded as the most modern of India's cities. It has large parks, wide streets, modern shops and many Internet cafés. Bangalore is India's high-tech centre, and it is famous for its computer and software industries, aircraft industries and its international **telecommunications** services.

Why tourists travel to India

Things to do and see

India is a fascinating country. It has become a place many people travel to for adventure. Tourists from all over the world visit India each year.

The Golden Triangle

Many visitors to India begin with 'The Golden Triangle'. The starting point is Delhi, then Agra, to see the famous Taj Mahal. The next stop is Jaipur; it is known as the 'Pink City' because its old buildings are a yellow-pink colour.

The River Ganges

Other visitors go to India to make a **pilgrimage** to the holy River Ganges. They take part in religious ceremonies and celebrations.

Beach holidays

For many travellers to India, Goa is the place to visit. Goa is very popular with tourists who want to lie on sandy beaches and swim in the warm waters of the Arabian Sea. Some take the opportunity to try water sports,

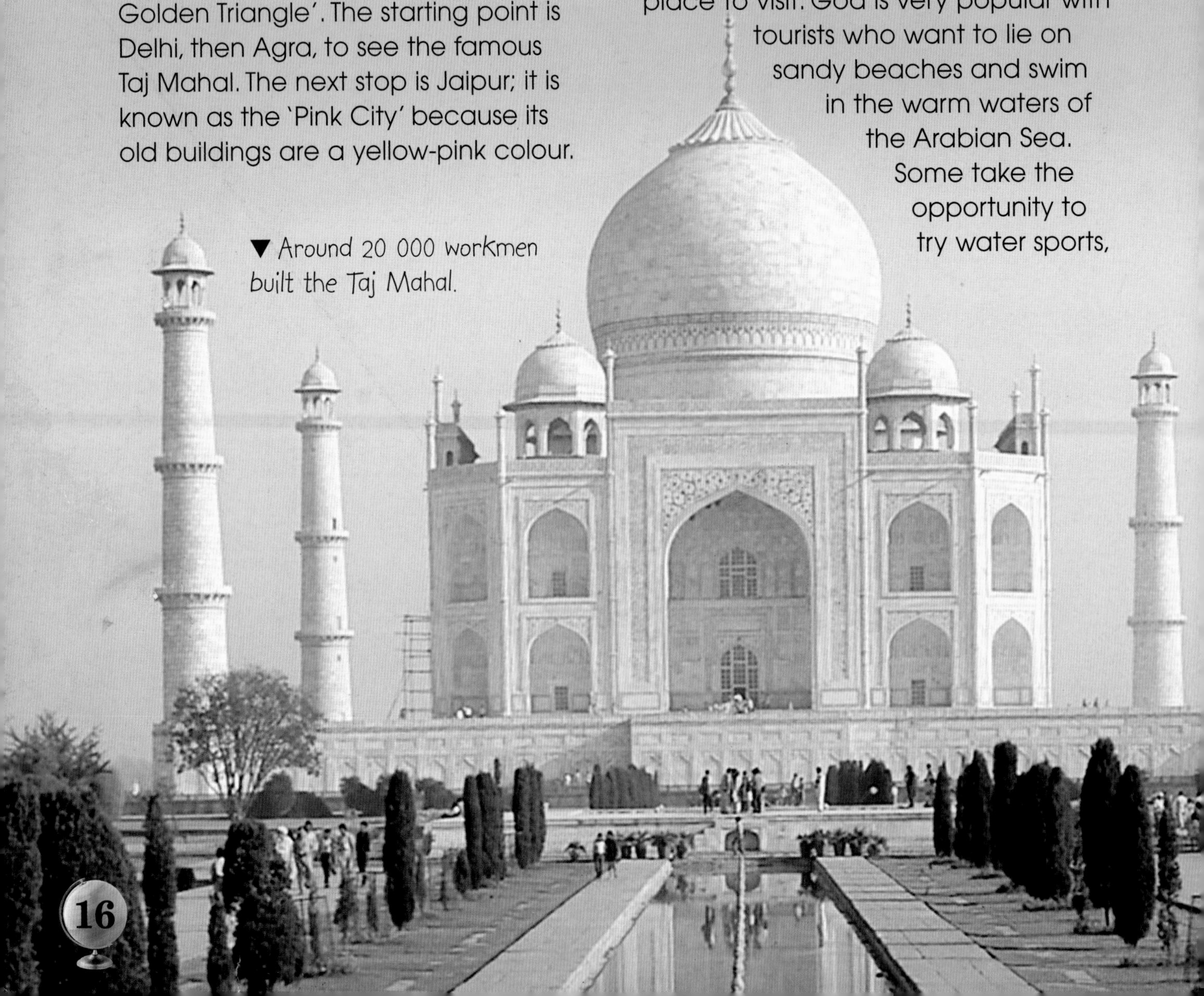

▼ Around 20 000 workmen built the Taj Mahal.

◀ Goa's beaches are fringed with palm trees. Early in the morning or late in the evening you will *see* fishermen on the beach hauling in their catch using sturdy ropes. They are very pleased if you lend a hand!

such as windsurfing and yachting. Others visit tiny fishing villages and wander around the colourful markets.

At the markets you can buy beautiful silks, carved figurines, silverware and brass, finely crafted jewellery and carpets. Bargaining about the prices with the market stallholders is part of the fun for tourists, and there are many fantastic bargains.

Amazing, but true!

The Taj Mahal at Agra took 23 years to build. It was built by Emperor Shah Jahan in memory of his second wife, Mumtaz Mahal. She died in 1630 while having a baby. It is said that the emperor was so heartbroken when his wife died that his hair turned grey overnight.

▼ Shawls, blankets and colourful fabrics can all be found in local markets.

Getting around India

On the move

India is a very large country and you will probably use different forms of transport to travel around. India is criss-crossed by the largest railway system in Asia.

▼ Most people do not own a car, so public transport of every sort is always much in demand.

Rickshaws

The **rickshaw** is the world's oldest form of wheeled transport. Millions of rickshaws are still in use in India today. They are used by businessmen going to work, children going to and from school, people going shopping and tourists, who enjoy the novelty of this cheap method of transport.

◄ Only in Kolkata are rickshaws still pulled by men. In other cities, bicycles are used to pull them.

India's busy roads

In the overcrowded cities and towns of India, you will be amazed at how busy the main roads are. They are crammed with cars, buses, lorries, rickshaws, ox-carts, bicycles and pedestrians, all competing for the limited space on the roads. High traffic levels have increased pollution in the cities. This is a serious environmental concern for the country.

In India's villages, where the standard of roads is poor and a car ride can be very bumpy, the locals often use ox-carts to travel around. The journey is slow but sure.

Read Geeta's diary extract of her first journey in a rickshaw.

Inside the rickshaw it was very hot, and our journey was slow, bumpy and noisy. The street was so busy with people, bicycles, other rickshaws, motorcycles, ox-carts, heavily laden lorries, cars, overcrowded buses (that had people hanging from the sides and roofs!), beggars and thin, hump-backed cows.

19

The River Ganges

India's great life source

If you journey along the length of the River Ganges, you will travel about 2478km across India into Bangladesh, where the river enters the Bay of Bengal. The river is the life source of the country. More than 350 million people use the waters of the River Ganges in their daily lives. The water is used in their homes for drinking, for cleaning and washing; in their factories; on their farms and as a means of transport.

The holy river

This river lies at the heart of India's religious beliefs. **Hindus** consider the river to be the goddess Ganga, and so its water is holy to them. All along the river there are **ghats**, where **pilgrims** can enter the river to bathe. People cremate (burn) their dead on its banks and throw the remains into the river in the belief that the goddess Ganga will take the dead to heaven.

▼ The holiest of India's cities is Varanasi, where thousands of pilgrims wash in the river while praying. Even in winter they brave the freezing temperatures.

▲ Saddhus are Hindu holy men who give up ordinary life and devote themselves to religious practice.

Read this extract from Anil's autobiography.

I was 11 years old when I first went to bathe in the River Ganges with my father. Early one morning we walked, with thousands of other Hindus, down to the bathing ghat. There we prayed, lit **diva lamps** and floated them down the river. Seeing the huge number of glowing diva lamps floating in the early morning mist is a sight I will never forget.

21

Travelling along the River Ganges

▶ Deforestation in northern India is causing serious soil erosion.

The journey begins

If you decide to travel the length of the River Ganges, your journey will begin at the **source** of the river at the Gangotri **glacier**, in the foothills of the Himalayas. As the Ganges runs through northern India, you will see how much this area has been affected by trees being cut down from the forests.

The Upper Ganges Canal

The Upper Ganges **Canal** takes water from the Ganges to **irrigate** farmland. This means that a second crop can be grown each year after the first crop has been watered by the rains of the **monsoon**.

Kanpur

Your next stop along the Ganges will be the industrial city of Kanpur. Here the leather and textile factories dump harmful wastes such as bleach, dye and chemicals into the river. This industrial pollution, added to the human **sewage** and the remains of bodies cremated on the riverbanks, makes the waters of the Ganges a serious health risk.

▼ River water is used to irrigate the rice paddies (fields) so that more crops can be grown.

Map labels: Gangotri Glacier, Bhagirathi, Haridwar, New Delhi, Upper Ganges Canal, Ganges, Agra, Kanpur, Yamuna, Ghaghara, CHINA, TIBET, Mt Everest, NEPAL, BHUTAN, Brahmaputra, Patna, Ganges, Varanasi, Allahabad, Ganges, Bhagalpur, Farakka Barrage, BANGLADESH, Son, Tropic of Cancer, Narmada, INDIA, Kolkata, Hooghly, Ganges Delta, Mahanadi, Bay of Bengal, 0 200 miles

The Silk City

The river flows on to Bhagalpur, the 'Silk City'. Silk is produced from the cocoons of the silkworm caterpillars. Much of the spinning is still done by hand.

The end of the journey

Just before the Ganges leaves India and forms its **delta** in Bangladesh, you will see the Farakka **Barrage** that was built to improve navigation to the port of Kolkata (Calcutta).

◄ Heavy pollution is a major health hazard.

Read this extract from a tourist's travel journal.

Impressions of northern India

In many places the trees had been cut down. Local people had taken some of the wood to use as fuel and building materials; but an international logging company which wanted to sell the timber had cut down most of the trees. During the last **monsoon** season a lot of the soil had been washed away because the trees could no longer protect the earth from the rains. There were no sounds of birds or animals.

23

Food – cooking and eating in India

▶ A street seller squeezes out coils of deliciously sweet jelebi mixture into bubbling oil.

My name is Srinvas. I live in southern India. We eat idlis (steamed rice cakes) and doshe (rice flour pancakes). I love bhujia and sambar (very hot vegetable stews) made with kerri (spicy sauces).

My name is Raju. I am a Sikh and I live in Punjab. I like to eat parathas (bread), lamb curry and potatoes cooked in spices.

My name is Suribi. I live in Goa. I like to eat Bombay duck. Bombay duck is not a duck! It is fish that is curried or fried.

My name is Nitan and I live in Kashmir. My favourite foods include rogan josh (curried lamb), koftas (spicy meatballs) and yakhni (stew of fennel seeds and curry spices).

Indian food

Indian food is colourful and uses many spices. Travelling around India you will eat different meals depending upon two things – what is grown in a particular region and the religion followed there. Many Indians are vegetarians. **Hindus** do not eat beef. **Muslims** do not eat pork.

How to eat

Even though knives and forks are used in India, eating with the fingers of your right hand shows good manners. You are able to feel and appreciate the texture of the food.

Indian sweets

Indian children love sweets. *Halva*, *ladoos* and *burfi* are delicious sweets made from milk products. Favourite drinks include *lassi* (a cold buttermilk drink), coconut milk and *chai* (tea). In large cities and towns, children also drink fizzy western drinks.

▲ Press the food firmly together between your fingers, then scoop it up to your mouth to eat.

▼ Market spices are sold by weight.

Visiting sacred places in India

Geeta's teacher asked her to find out about Indian religions and special holy places while she was visiting her grandparents in Mumbai. Read the extracts from her travel notebook.

Islam
Interesting facts
* Followers of Islam are called **Muslims**.
* The Qur'an is the holy book of Islam.
* Muslims believe the Qur'an contains the exact words that Allah (God) said to **Mohammed**, his **prophet** on Earth.
* Muslims worship in places called **mosques**.
* During prayers, parts of the Qur'an are read five times a day.

PLACE TO VISIT
Kashmir is an important Islamic region.

Buddhism
Interesting facts
* Many followers of Buddhism live in remote areas of the Himalayas.
* Some **Buddhists** originally came from Tibet, which is to the north of India.
* Buddhists believe in a peaceful existence and never cause harm to any living things.
* Buddhists paint prayers on cloths, which are known as prayer flags. These are hung from cords and stretched out like washing lines across the sky, because Buddhists hope the prayers will travel with the wind.

PLACE TO VISIT
The monastery at Leh, in Ladakh, which is in the far north of India.

▼ The Buddhist monastery at Leh in Ladakh.

▶ The Golden Temple is built on a beautiful pool. Visitors must take off their shoes.

▶ Hindus offer sticks of incense, sweets and flowers to their gods.

Sikhism

Interesting facts
* Sikhism includes elements from both Hinduism and Islam.
* The holy book is called Guru Granth Sahib. It is kept at the Golden Temple.
* **Sikh** men must never cut the hair on their face or head. They wear their hair coiled under a turban.

PLACE TO VISIT
Golden Temple (Gurdawa) in Amritsar, Punjab.

Hinduism

Interesting facts
* Eighty per cent of the Indian population follow the Hindu religion.
* **Hindus** believe that Hindu gods and goddesses represent the different qualities and powers of the one supreme God.
* Hindus believe that the gods and goddesses live in **temples** and **shrines**.
* Hindus have many festivals and celebrations, for example Diwali and Holi.
* Hindus believe that the place where any rivers meet is sacred. Stepped platforms, called **ghats**, are built to enable pilgrims to bathe more easily in the River Ganges.

PLACE TO VISIT
Allahabad, where the River Ganges, River Yamuna and the mythical River Saraswati meet, is the holiest place on Earth for Hindus to bathe.

▶ A Hindu girl makes an offering to the gods.

Glossary

barrage
a structure or bridge in a river that directs water in a particular direction

Buddhists
followers of a religion of India and Asia

canal
a man-made waterway

continent
one of Earth's seven large landmasses

deforestation
when trees or forests are cut down

delta
a flat area where a river meets the sea

diva lamps
small, bowl-shaped containers, sometimes clay, with oil inside and a single wick that is set alight

exporter
a person or company who sells things abroad

ghats
platforms or wide steps on an Indian riverbank that provide access to the water

glacier
a slow-moving mass of ice and snow

Hindus
followers of one of the main religions of India

industries
groups of companies that make a particular thing, such as steel

irrigation
bringing water to land for farming

Mohammed
the Prophet of Islam

monsoon
the annual wet season lasting 3-4 months

mosques
places where Muslims gather and pray

Muslims
followers of the Islamic religion

ox (*plural form:* oxen)
an animal like a cow that is used on farms

pilgrimage
a journey taken for spiritual purposes

pilgrims
people on a pilgrimage

rickshaw
a small vehicle pulled by a person or a bicycle

rural
of the countryside

sacred
viewed as holy by a religion

sewage
waste material from toilets

shrines
small temples that honour a particular god or holy person

Sikhs
followers of Sikhism, a religion of India

slums
very poor areas of a city

soil erosion
when soil is washed away

source
the place where a river starts

telecommunications
telephone, radio and television networks

temples
places where Hindus and Buddhists pray

terraced
hillside cut into a series of flat levels

urban
of the town or city

Index

Teaching ideas and activities for children

The following activities address and develop the geographical 'enquiry' approach, and promote thinking skills and creativity. The activities in section A have been devised to help children develop higher order thinking, based on Bloom's taxonomy of thinking. The activities in section B have been devised to promote different types of learning styles, based on Howard Gardner's theory of multiple intelligences.

A: ACTIVITIES TO DEVELOP THINKING SKILLS

ACTIVITIES TO PROMOTE RESEARCH AND RECALL OF FACTS

Ask the children to:

• make an alphabet book for a young child, illustrating the contrasts in India.

• research and investigate a mountain environment (the Himalayas). The children could present their information in a poster or a Powerpoint presentation.

ACTIVITIES TO PROMOTE UNDERSTANDING

Ask the children to replicate a simple A3 map or picture of India. Place the children in groups of four to six. Tell them they are going to reproduce the map or picture you have. In their groups, ask them to number themselves and to discuss strategies they could use to reproduce your picture. Call each number, one at a time, to look at the picture for two minutes. Then ask them to go back and draw what they can remember, while discussing the picture and strategies with their group..Give the children five minutes to do this. Then call the next member of the group, and so on. At the end, show the children the original and ask them to evaluate each group's work.

ACTIVITIES TO PROMOTE THE USE OF KNOWLEDGE AND SKILLS TO SOLVE PROBLEMS

Ask the children to:

• find out, by using reference books or the Internet, how to make a chapatti or a diva lamp and to write instructions to show this.

• make notes to explain the reasons why the streets in Indian cities are so polluted and congested.